Everyone Has Something

Abby's Story

by

Abigail M. Ferraro

Images at the beginning of each chapter and on the last page were created by Kerry Ferraro.
Cover photo by Eric Reppert
Author photo on back cover by Emily Ellsworth

*Dedicated to everybody who supports me
and to all the kids with arthritis, Crohn's, or uveitis*

*All money raised from this book goes to Abby's Army,
a 501(c)(3) tax-exempt organization.*

Disclaimer from Abby's mom: I'm so proud of Abby for writing this book. These are her words, and I don't want to change any of them. I do feel like I need to make a disclaimer. Obviously, after having near constant nausea and other symptoms for three and a half years, she has very strong, positive feelings towards the medicine that has helped her feel better. Those feelings obviously came through in the book. While Humira appears to be the right choice for Abby, it is not right for everyone. Please follow your doctor's recommendations.

Chapter 1

The Problem

Hi! My name is Abby Ferraro, and I'm in third grade at Shady Grove Elementary School. I have juvenile idiopathic arthritis in my right ankle and right pinky toe and my right knee. I also have Crohn's disease and have uveitis in my left eye. I'll tell you about my problem and my solution. Before I started Humira, I had a lot of uveitis flares, ankle and pinky toe flares, and my belly bothered me (a lot sometimes) because of my Crohn's disease. A flare is when my pain, nausea, and swelling get worse. Sometimes I even had to sit out of gym if one of my body parts bothered me. My belly kept me up at night, sometimes until midnight. It was hard to sleep when it bothered me. On car rides, the bumps, sways, and dips bothered my stomach, too. On the way to my school, there is a tickle bump, and Mom has to go slow when we go over it so it does not bother my stomach, especially on days my belly is bothering me a lot.

Before I started Humira, I also had a lot of belly pain and nausea. I had to miss school and camp sometimes because it was bothering me that much. I also missed gymnastics classes and took a break from dance. I skipped some play dates because I wasn't feeling up to it. I didn't want to, but Mom made me. Over by my grandma's house, they have a Halloween parade, but I haven't been able to go in three years.

Mom, me, and Dad on vacation

Me and my dogs, Lilah and Max

Chapter 2

All I Went Through: Belly Problems

My belly problems started in March 2015 after food poisoning on vacation. I thought having to miss the Bibbidi Bobbidi Boutique and eating at Be Our Guest was bad enough, but it was just the start. About 3 weeks later, I started having a lot of belly pains. I had a bunch of blood work, urine and stool samples, x-rays, and a breath test. They were all REALLY ANNOYING. My first gastroenterologist (GI doctor) dismissed me. He said that sometimes kids, normally girls, just have unexplained belly pains, but that I'll get over it. He said I had irritable bowel syndrome (IBS), and he wouldn't schedule another appointment even though I was hurting more than when I started seeing him. Before my belly started hurting, I was bigger than 25% of the kids my age. After six months, I was only bigger than 9% of the kids.

My parents took me to see a different GI doctor. She helped me feel a little better, but I still had pains. She gave me more x-rays and blood work and had me try a bunch of medicines. One of the medicines made me feel like I was spinning around when I was trying to sleep. My parents had me try a bunch of diets, and I stopped eating some foods. None of the diets helped.

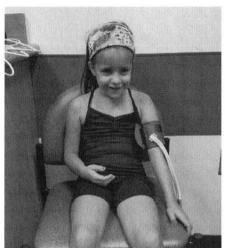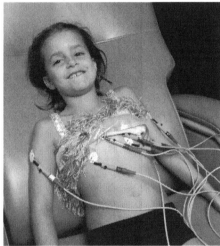

I had a lot of doctor appointments and had to get an EKG before starting one medicine (they don't hurt at all)

Sometimes, when my belly bothered me for almost the whole week, I felt like I wouldn't ever have a day where my belly felt better. Mom and Dad would snuggle me and give me a heating pad. They gave me some medicines that helped a little, like gripe water, Pedialax, or gas drops. I'm lucky to have medicines that helped a little. Some people don't have anything that helps them feel better. Mom always says that everyone has something. She's right. Everyone has problems. I have friends who don't have enough money for some place nice or safe to live or

5

for food. I have friends whose parents are divorced or not around or are sick. I have friends with other medical problems. Everyone has something. Mom used to use tattoo pens to write on my belly. She would write "Today will be a better day." Whenever I needed something to help me get through school, I would just lift up my shirt and read it. She also would write "strong" and "brave" on my arm to remind me that I was both.

Time passed, I wasn't getting better and stopped gaining weight, so my parents decided to try ANOTHER GI doctor. This new doctor wanted to do more tests. First, I had an upper GI with small bowel follow through. That's a big name, but all I had to do was get MORE x-rays and drink very gross stuff that made me feel like I was going to vomit. I didn't like that. Then I had to do an upper endoscopy. Mom told them she wanted me to also have a colonoscopy. I was mad at Mom for that. The colonoscopy prep was bad. All I remember of the tests is going to sleep and waking up. I woke up too early and tried to pull out my IV and was freaking out. It scared Dad. Hahaha. Two days later, they called Mom and said I was diagnosed with Crohn's disease. I started Pentasa the next day. That was in June 2018. More than three years after my belly started bothering me. Three years, people! THREE! I finally had a diagnosis and medicine that helped a little.

I've talked about Crohn's or Crohn's disease a lot. I'm going to stop really quickly and explain what it is in case you don't know. Crohn's disease isn't contagious. It's an autoimmune disease, which means my immune system fights my body instead of fighting germs. With Crohn's disease, my immune system attacks the part of my body that digests food. It gives me mouth ulcers and makes my intestines swell, which causes the belly pains and nausea. Now, I'll get back to my story.

 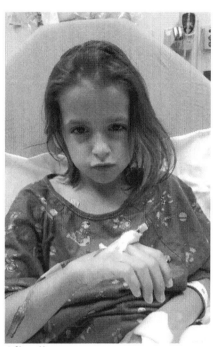

No more Pentasa! Yay!   After the scopes

Because of where the Crohn's was, I had to get something called an MRE to see if there was Crohn's in my small intestines. I had to drink a milkshake that I really liked. Yum, yum. They started an IV, which I hated. Then I had an MRI, which takes pictures of the inside of your body like an x-ray. It wasn't as easy as an x-ray. I was in a loud machine. I wore earplugs, but they didn't work. My foot fell asleep, but I couldn't move. The noise overwhelmed me, which made my belly bother me. Then they injected contrast into my IV, but they didn't warn me about how it would feel. It felt really weird and cold, and it burned at the same time. It scared me a lot, and Mommy had to hold my hand.

My parents switched me to the IBD clinic and my fourth GI doctor. Yay! They are nicest doctors ever! They are the ones who prescribed the medicine that has helped me to feel so much better. I'll get to that later in the book.

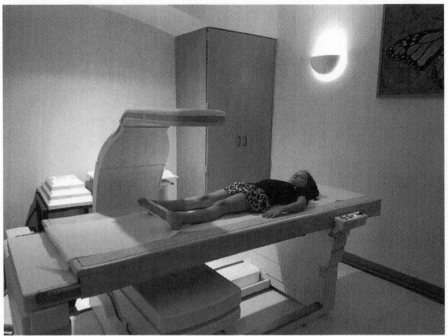

I needed a bone density scan after I was diagnosed with Crohn's. They are easy peasy.

Chapter 3

All I Went Through: JIA

All of my doctor appointments didn't start because of my belly. I've been going to a pediatrician, rheumatologist, ophthalmologist, and allergist for forever. When I was 19 months old, my right knee swelled a lot. I don't remember this, but Mom and Dad do. They took me to the pediatrician who sent me for blood work and x-rays. Doctors sure do need a LOT of blood work. After all the tests told them what I didn't have, they still didn't know what I did have. I ended up getting MORE blood work. Then I got more blood work and more x-rays. Then I ended up at an orthopedist who sent me to a rheumatologist. He diagnosed me with oligoarticular juvenile idiopathic arthritis (JIA) with flares in my right knee, right ankle, and right pinky toe. He put me on a type of medicine called NSAIDs.

I'll stop again to explain what juvenile idiopathic arthritis is. It is another autoimmune disease, like Crohn's, except my immune system attacks my joints, tendons, and eyes.

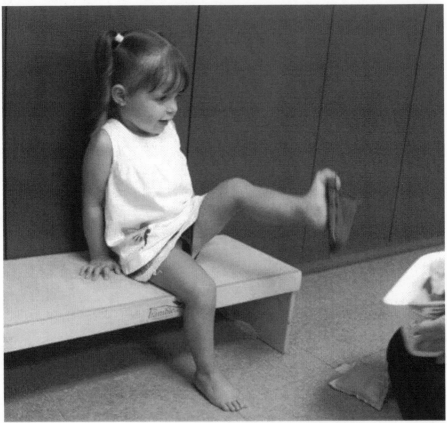

I needed a lot of physical therapy when I was first diagnosed. I need PT and OT again. They make it really fun.

I was really lucky. A lot of my friends with JIA took a lot longer than a month to get diagnosed. The rheumy (that's what we call rheumatologists sometimes to make it easier) took some fluid out of my knee and gave me a steroid shot in it while I was awake. I was only 21 months old, and I was afraid of needles for a while afterwards. Mom had to keep telling me that it's a small needle and won't hurt like when they stuck the big needle in my knee. I've gotten a lot better. I was also scared to go into parking garages, because all the doctors and tests. When Mom took me to the mall, I was even scared because we parked in a garage. Afraid of a mall! Can you believe that? I LOVE shopping!

Mom took me to a different rheumy a few months later. I loved my new rheumy. He was nice and funny and did lots of great tricks. My JIA ended up being in remission for a while. Yay!!!!!! I had a few times where my joints would hurt, but nothing lasted too long until this year. My right ankle started hurting a lot at the beginning of the year. It would take a long time to loosen up in the morning. The NSAIDs were hurting my belly and Tylenol only helped a little. My rheumatologist, the one I've been seeing for six years, didn't think it was my JIA and was talking to Mom about something called AMPS. A month after my appointment, my right foot and ankle swelled. My normal rheumy couldn't see me, so I saw someone else who works with him. They said that I had tendonitis from either the Crohn's or JIA or both. I liked this rheumy so much that we're making him my new rheumy. He even emailed Mom to see if I was feeling any better. Mom works with him on PR-COIN projects, which I think is pretty cool. (PR-COIN is the Pediatric Rheumatology Care and Outcomes Improvement Network. You can learn more about it at pr-coin.org)

Me and my new rheumatologist, Dr. Sandy Burnham

Chapter 4

All I Went Through: Uveitis

When I was first diagnosed with JIA, I had to start seeing an ophthalmologist (eye doctor). The JIA can cause uveitis. With uveitis, the body attacks the eyes instead of attacking the joints like it does in arthritis. I've gone there for almost all of my life (before I was two!). I was good for six years. One day, my eyes started to get really red and itchy and they hurt. I couldn't see out of my left eye that well and light hurt my eye (that's called light sensitivity). My eye doctor was on vacation, so Mom took me to hers. He diagnosed me with uveitis. I was very scared and cried. I called Daddy, and he skipped his meeting because his baby girl was scared. He came to cheer me up.

The reason I was scared was because my friend Joy had uveitis and is now blind from it. I was afraid that might happen to me. Mommy made me feel better by telling me that back when Joy was diagnosed they didn't have

13

medicine to help her, but I got medicine right away. Yay! Mom told me that I was lucky that I had symptoms. Most kids don't have symptoms with uveitis.

I started eye drops and went to see my regular eye doctor after she came back from vacation. My uveitis was cleared up from the eye drops. The eye doctor didn't believe me. Grrr. She said kids don't have symptoms with uveitis and that I just wanted glasses. Mom was not happy with her and neither was I. Mom called her after my appointment. Then my parents took me to a uveitis specialist. She is very, very, very nice.

Ready for my eye exam with Curious George

The uveitis came back a few times. My uveitis specialist put me on steroid eye drops each time. The eye drops helped a lot. When I was on the eye drops, my eye pressure went up. They had to do extra pressure tests where they numb my eye. I did not like those tests. They are the worst eye tests ever. After I started Humira and stopped the eye drops, my eye pressure went back down. Yay! No more of the numbing eye drops.

Chapter 5

The Solution

This past August, all of my doctors got together to talk about how to help me. They prescribed Humira shots to help with my Crohn's, JIA, and uveitis. I've taken what they call loading doses and two regular doses so far. The first two doses were the loading doses because the shots had a lot more medicine in them than my regular shots will. Now, I'll have the less medicine all the time. Yay! After Mom gave me my first Humira shot, Dad told me that she was more scared to give me the shot than I was to get the shot. I didn't believe him. I didn't think that Mom would be scared, but she said that she was. That surprised me a lot.

After that first Humira shot, I felt GREAT the next morning! Before, when I said I felt great, I thought I did, but I didn't. After my shot, I stopped taking my Pentasa, cyproheptadine (another belly medicine), and my steroid eye drops. I hope to wean off my fludrocortisone soon. I take that one for my low blood pressure. I also took off my KT tape, which I was wearing because I had an ankle flare that caused tendonitis, but after the Humira shot my ankle felt better. My ankle always hurt when I used the spring board in gymnastics, but now it doesn't. Now, I am not sitting out of gym class either. When Mom drove me to school and went over the tickle bump, I didn't even feel it! I get the shot every two weeks. I am so happy that my Humira shot helped me feel better.

My mouth sores and eczema cleared up, and I need less sleep now, too. I was sleeping 11 to 11-½ hours every night. I'd start getting ready for bed at 7:30pm and Mom would wake me up for school at 7:30am so I could get to school on time. Now, I'm only sleeping about ten hours a night. Some days, I have time to read in bed, do my PT and OT exercises, and practice my music before school.

I still have a little nausea and belly pain around three days a week, but not as bad as before. I also am happy that I have a brave mom and supportive family to help me get me through hard, scary, and even difficult times. I have the best family ever! I am so glad to have them by my side every step of the way. I still have to go to my doctors to make sure everything is okay. I go to the eye doctor, GI doctor, and rheumatologist. I have to get blood work every three months to check that I'm on the right dose of Humira, to make sure I'm not creating antibodies to it (that would mean my body is trying to fight off the Humira instead of letting it work like it's supposed to), and to make sure the Humira isn't hurting me. I'm not happy about that.

I still get scared before my shot, but I'm getting better. The shots also hurt less each time because I'm getting less medicine. The first two shots hurt more than my last two shots, but none of the shots were too bad. Even though I'm scared and the shots hurt, I'm glad I get the shot. I am so happy to have a medicine that finally makes me feel better.

After Humira at Skyzone

Chapter 6

The Good Stuff

I'm not happy about having arthritis, but I'm happy about the good stuff I get to do because of my arthritis. I get to go to the Arthritis Foundation's Juvenile Arthritis Conferences and JA Family Days. The JA Conference is where all the kids who have arthritis and their parents come together. Parents go to grown up sessions while kids go to kid sessions. We learn about arthritis and have special guests. The special guests have arthritis, too. Some of the stuff we do in our kid sessions includes seeing therapy dogs, yoga, dance, scavenger hunts, music therapy, arts and crafts, and obstacle courses. We learn about advocacy, our diet and why it's important, our emotions, and how to talk about our diseases. They give us fun little packets that we get to take home. Every opening night of the JA Conference, we have a dinner and people get up and talk. They always have something fun like someone singing or dancing or performing.

The sorority Alpha Omicron Pi gives each kid at the conference a stuffed panda. Every kid gets a stuffed panda. Even the siblings of the JIA kids get them, because JIA is hard on the whole family. I have a panda from every conference I went to. I sleep with the panda pillow pet I got at the Seattle conference. It's my favorite.

Me with the AOII mascot

The best thing about JA Conferences is the friends. You get to meet new friends and see old ones. I'm friend with a lot of kids with JIA and their families. Some of my best friends from conferences are Tory, Mariah, Mauriauna, Tina, Kiki, Megan, Kate, Melanie, Carmen, Piper, Anjie, Laura, Erin, and the list could go on, but then this book would be huge.

My friends help me even when I'm not at conference. When I was scared to take Humira, Melanie video called me. Melanie takes Humira, too. She let me watch her seven year old daughter Megan give her the shot.

JA Conferences are for everyone in the United States, and JA Family Days are local. We have snacks, and there's a service dog in training that comes in. They brought in a light switch and had him turn the light on and off. It was cool. We play lots of games, and we have yoga. Our JA Family Day is in a place with a pool. I always go swimming after the JA Family Day.

JA Conferences have allowed me to visit cool landmarks and monuments. In D.C., I saw the Lincoln Memorial, Washington Monument and the reflecting pool (It was green and ducks were swimming in it. YUCK!). I also toured the White House and the US Capitol. I saw the World War II Memorial and toured museums. I cartwheeled around D.C. In Indianapolis, I saw the Zoo and the State fair. I got a cool plucky instrument. In Washington state, I went up in the Seattle Space Needle. It was 605 feet tall. I leaned on the glass, but Mom didn't want to (I think she's afraid of heights). We saw the Chihuly Garden and Glass, and we went to the aquarium. When the conference was in Florida, I got to go to the Bibbidi Bobbidi Boutique since I wasn't able to go when I was there on vacation because I had food poisoning. My belly was bothering me when we were at the JA Conference, so we didn't do any rides. I was in Disney World, and I couldn't do any rides! Worst thing ever!

At the top of the Space Needle

With Dad (in his Abby's Army shirt!) at Chihuly Garden and Glass

Cartwheeling in front of the Washington Monument

Mariah, Mauriauna, Hayley, Me, and Addie at the Space Needle

Chapter 7

Advocacy Rules!

When I was six, I started to advocate with the Arthritis Foundation, and I love it. I get to talk to lawmakers in D.C. and Harrisburg, PA, about arthritis, and I learn what to say. I say, "Hello, my name is Abigail Ferraro, and I have juvenile idiopathic arthritis in my knee, ankle, and pinky toe. I was diagnosed with JIA when I was 20 months old, and there are 300,000 kids in the US with arthritis. Will you advocate for us?" After I'm done talking, Mom tells them what they should do to help people with arthritis. Mom says before I started doing this, I was very shy—up the butt shy (that means I would bury my face in Mom's butt to hide), but now I'm not. I'm happy that I can advocate for the kids who aren't able to do it for themselves.

In Harrisburg, I've met with Representative Harper, Senator Greenleaf's staff, and Senator Schwank's staff. In D.C., I've had meetings with the staff of Senator Casey,

Senator Toomey, Representative Boyle, Representative Doyle, Representative Rothfus, and Representative Dent.

Advocating with the Arthritis Foundation has also taught me how to advocate for myself in school and at my activities.

My JIA friends in front of the Capitol (Me, Tory, Mariah, Tina, and Mauriauna)

Chapter 8

What I Learned

I learned that Anjie's husband has a really good beard.

Everyone has something. Never think someone has it better than you, because you just don't know what their something is.

If your doctor doesn't believe you, or isn't helping, find a different doctor.

Sometimes tests don't tell you what you have. It's okay if they just tell you what you don't have. It still gets you closer to an answer.

People you only see once or twice a year can still be the best friends ever.

Stressing about something doesn't help. It only makes you feel worse.

Things are never as bad as you expect.

If it's something that makes you feel better, but it hurts, it's still worth it.

I learned how do magic tricks from my doctor.

You should speak up for yourself and to help others. Some people don't like speaking up for themselves, so you should. Make yourself be heard.

When you advocate, you can make a difference.

I learned all sorts of medical words, like ileocecal valve, and learned how to spell big words like rheumatologist, juvenile idiopathic arthritis, physical therapy, and colonoscopy.

Exercise makes you feel better. It helps my arthritis and my Crohn's.

Some food can make you feel bad. Even if you like it, you should stop eating it. You don't want to risk getting sick.

Things will always get better. Sometimes it takes a while to get better, but it's worth the wait.

Service dogs are very important. You should never pet one when it's working.

I'm lucky because I have medicine that helps me and a lot of kids don't.

Anjie's husband's beard (Mom says his name is Shawn)

Symptoms are good. They tell you something is wrong. I'm really lucky that I had symptoms for uveitis. Most times people don't get symptoms with uveitis.

I'm lucky because I have a school with a nice principal and teachers.

Some kids feel different because they have arthritis. They're afraid to talk to other kids, but I think they should speak up.

Doctors are very important.

Germs are really bad if you're taking Humira.

Kids with arthritis or who have anything like I have should speak up for themselves.

Thank You!

Chapter 9

So Thankful

Thank you to my family. When things are tough, they always stand by my side every step of the way. If I'm scared, they are always there to protect me and help me. I want to thank Mom for being so brave to give me my Humira shot, and thank Daddy for being brave, as well, because he didn't like to see his little girl hurt.

Thank you to my grandma for taking the train home when we both had doctor appointments and mom couldn't drive her home after her appointment.

Thanks to my friends who help when I'm at school. When I don't feel good, they ask me what's wrong and help me get through a lot of things. Annabel, Lily, Tori, and Elisia are awesome. When I wasn't feeling well, I had to cancel playdates. They weren't mad at me. They just scheduled more playdates.

Thank you to all of my Abby's Army supporters. Every year, I win a medal at the Philadelphia Walk to Cure Arthritis because of all of the money I raise for people with arthritis. I couldn't do that without all of the people who donate money and who come to my walk to support me. The money we raise at the walk helps the Arthritis Foundation do all the great things I talked about.

Me with my medal for raising the most money two years ago

Thanks to my JIA friends for helping me get through tough times.

A ginormous thank you to Tory, Mariah, Mauriauna, and Tina for helping me when I was scared. At the JA conferences, they play with me when Mom has to go to a meeting. They take me to their room or walk around the hotel and explore and play games. Another thank you to Tina for letting me pick on her. Another thank you to Tory for proofreading my book.

Thank you to my babysitter Kathy. When I had to get my first Humira shot, I had to wait an hour while my parents had training. An hour, people! Just waiting. Thinking about my shot. She stayed with me and watched me play Roblox. When I had my first flare, I had to go to physical therapy (PT) to make my ankle and everything stronger. Kathy used to take me. I have sleepovers at her house and her dog is so stinkin' cute.

Thank you to Melanie. When I was scared to take Humira, she video called me and let her seven year old daughter give her the shot. I was still scared, but only a little scared. She helped me a lot.

I have the best principal! Thank you to Dr. Albanese for helping me bring my backpack to my room when I had my arthritis flare. He raced me up the steps and always makes sure we're safe. He's the one who said that I need a 504 plan. A lot of other schools aren't good about that.

I LOVE gymnastics and the piano!

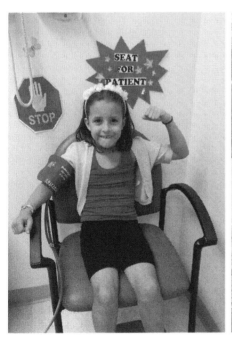

Thank you to all my teachers at Shady Grove. My teachers last year, Mrs. Rookstool, and this year, Mrs. Pascucci, let me go to the bathroom and nurse whenever I need to. They let me put my head down or sit in the quiet hall when I need to. They are the best teachers I ever had. Mrs. Pascucci even proofread this book for me! Thank you!

Thank you to Mr. D for letting me sit out of gym whenever I needed to. He never makes me feel bad about it.

Thank you to Michelle Wade for being the best pediatrician EVER! Thank you for never dismissing me and always believing what I say. And thank you for never giving up and for being you.

Thank you to Dr. Esi Morgan for creating PR-COIN and for Dr. Sandy Burnham for bringing PR-COIN to CHOP. They want to make all the kids with JIA better. (PR-COIN is the Pediatric Rheumatology Care and Outcomes Improvement Network.)

Thanks you to all my doctors for helping me get through everything that has been so tough and scary. Thank you for helping me get better. The doctors who didn't listen to me really make me glad for the ones who do listen to me.

Thanks to the Arthritis Foundation for all the good stuff you do for kids with arthritis and for trying to find a cure.

Thank you to Miss Jamie and Miss Amy from Institute of Dance Artistry (IDA) in Fort Washington. When I wanted them to come to teach dance at the JA Conference when it was in Philly, they came and did it just for me. They also let me take a break from dance when I didn't feel up to finishing the year of dance. P.S. You're two of my favorite teachers.

Thank you Little Gym of Spring House for letting me leave early if my belly or ankle or anything wasn't quite right. Thank you for being goofy and making me forget about my belly. P.S. Gymnastics is my favorite sport.

Thank you to Anjie for proofreading my book.

Thank you to Theraplay for helping me to get my muscles stronger. I love all my therapists. They are all so nice and kind and generous.

A big thank you to YOU for reading my book.

By: Abigail Marie Ferraro, 8 years old

Raising awareness with Mom

And now some words from Mom...

Abby started writing this book because I asked her to make a video of what it was like before she started to feel better. My thought was that I would be able to show her the video in the future if she begins rebelling against taking her medicines. Often, kids will forget what it was like before they started feeling better and decide that they don't need their medicines anymore. Unfortunately, with biologics, once you stop taking a medicine, it won't always work when you try to start it up again. I wanted something she could look back on to remember what all she went through before she found her "magic" medicine. Once she started making the video, she discovered she had a lot to say. After her second video, she sat down and started typing.

I want to point out that the medicine is not a cure. She still has JIA and Crohn's disease. There is no cure for either. The medicine weakens her immune system to keep it from attacking her joints, eyes, and digestive system. The weakened immune system puts her at risk for infections, but we feel the benefits greatly outweigh the risks associated with the medicine. Also, although the medicine appears to be working for her now, that doesn't mean it will always work for her.

People who know Abby's story were aware of the amount of time it took to get her Crohn's diagnosis, but most weren't aware of the number of doctors it took to get there. Finding a doctor you trust and who listens to your child is an amazing thing. If you don't have both of those or if you are struggling to get answers to symptoms your child is having, please, get a second or third, or even a fourth, opinion.

Abby is one of the lucky ones. While she has a lot of stuff going on, she has relatively mild cases of all of them. She knows that. She sees the kids at the JA Conferences who have more severe symptoms. Those kids are why she started advocating. She didn't start advocating for herself. She faced her shyness and started advocating so she could help the other kids who weren't as fortunate as she was. Advocating for others allowed her to find her voice and own her story.

Thank you for reading her story. Thank you for supporting her and for being part of Abby's Army.

- Kerry (Abby's mom)

Someone I Love Has JUVENILE ARTHRITIS

Made in the USA
Middletown, DE
16 January 2019